I0572641

What We Hold On To

Poems of Coping, Connection, and Carrying On

The Chaos Section Poetry Project
Austin, TX

2026

Cover Artwork:
Turning Partly Cloudy by Midday by Bonner Fowles (acrylic on canvas)
Interior Artwork:
Warm, Warmer by Phoebe Shade (digital/mixed media illustration)
Planting in the Garden by Isabelle Luebke (graphite on paper)
Editors: Nick Allison and Rachel Armes-McLaughlin

ISBN: 979-8-9993042-2-3

First published: January 2026

Published by: The Chaos Section Press
Austin, Texas

thechaossectionpoetryproject.com

Dedication

For every artist who turns pain into meaning, who creates light from
what they've endured, and who reminds others they're not alone.

"As small groups of humans, it's hard to have much impact on the shape of things globally. You control what you can and double-down on beauty so you're not just being pounded by existential crisis."

— Jeff Tweedy

"There is a crack in everything, that's how the light gets in."

—Leonard Cohen, "Anthem"

Table of Contents

Introduction

Dear Readers,

I have been both excited and nervous about writing this introduction. When co-editor and fellow poet Nick Allison asked me if I wanted to write it, I thought, "Sure! But, what do I write?"

I feel like today is a good day to draft something. The words have started to come to me a few times now, but they haven't always felt…hopeful. And that's okay. After all, I have felt—like many of us —incredibly discouraged lately by the state of our nation under Donald Trump's authoritarian rule. Understandably. There is, and should be, a place for those feelings in writing. But today is November 5, 2025. It is exactly one year after Trump was devastatingly elected for a second time, true, but it is also one day after historic U.S. elections, where Democrats swept the board in open rejection of authoritarianism. This includes Democratic victories in right-leaning Georgia, with Peter Hubbard and Alicia Johnson defeating two Republican incumbents on the Public Service Commission—the first time in nearly 20 years that a Democrat won a statewide constitutional office in the state. And, oh, the hope I have seen pouring out of people today. Hope!

This brings me to the current Chaos Section Poetry Project theme: coping mechanisms. When everything is heavy—when the hits just keep coming, and it feels like things are spiraling beyond repair— coping becomes difficult. More than difficult, sometimes. And let's be real: the situation is still dire. Along with the wins we had this week, we have also seen the cessation of the Supplemental Nutrition Assistance Program (SNAP), with millions of Americans struggling to put food on the table. Not only that, we have seen the current administration openly admit their plans to defy a court order to release SNAP benefits. And the payments that did go out this month? Take them back, the administration said. Not to mention, we are staring down the barrel of a health insurance crisis (okay, okay, I guess I mentioned it). Meanwhile, ICE continues its destruction, and a thousand other issues remain. And heaven forbid any of us have personal life issues amid all this chaos (insert crazed laughter here).

So, it isn't any wonder that people far and wide are struggling to cope. Maybe you're eating too much junk. Maybe you can't sleep. Maybe you had a few too many drinks a few too many times. But maybe you are also spending time with your family and friends— playing board games, going on crisp walks, saying no to people and things that don't align with your values. Maybe you are writing poetry, like us and the other poets in this book. Perhaps you've done a little bit of all these things or their ilk.

While we grieve the many atrocities happening, we also celebrate the slow progress we make. Moments of collective hope, like we experienced this week, give us all a much-needed boost and hopefully help us cope with this nightmare in healthy ways. Glo Atanmo, business and storytelling coach, has a quote that I love: "Micro joys are how we survive macro grief." We need these hopeful moments to rest and revive. To survive.

Because this is a marathon, not a sprint.

Rachel Armes-McLaughlin
Little Rock, Arkansas
Winter 2025

What We Hold On To

When the World Tilts

Audrey Howitt

like now,
when toy soldiers cannot graze the sun
or crease skin,
I come home, to sand and mist,
to the way my eyes hold a horizon
knowing its impermanence against movement
its sturdiness
as planted feet hold the setting sun below water.

I want to know how we came to this,
though that won't take the pain away
or cause the sun to find its niche again.
I only write one word at a time
weigh out meaning, each against that horizon
and against feet that feel sand,
know its shifts as I rock back and forth
trying to change my view.

I Say the Words and Dance

Merril D. Smith

> *"Do not obey in advance."*
> —Timothy Snyder, *On Tyranny: Twenty Lessons from the Twentieth Century*

When they ban the books
and suppress the press—

I'll whisper the words
lest you forget

the world's not flat,
there are still facts,

there is still this,
despite the that.

For now, I titter at the naked king,
percolate slogans,
salt the air with slashing syllables and phrases,
ruminate,

Nolite te Bastardes Carborundorum

Jubilate.

For now, I'll laugh with you
and dance in the rain,

then dance some more for blue of sky
and for all the whens, despite the whys.

For now, I sip a fine Rhone red,
not to forget, to celebrate

how the grape lives on—transformed
as love is in memory.

For now, I'll shout the call,
the world is on fire,
resist, rebel,

but seed my words so they will bloom
fragrant, alluring—but jaggedly thorned.

The Order of Things

Meridith Allison

I've retreated from the world,
from the fractious unfolding of things,
and set my sights instead on all that is,
or ever was, or ever will be–

these motes of dust suspended in the morning light,
and the crumbs behind the toaster,
dog hair on the floor,
chaos at home as it is in the heavens.

The nerve to think I might prevail!
Even so–

I scour the sinks, wash the windows,
wipe baseboards and blinds.
I clean the top of the fridge, behind the books,
the grout, the filters, the fans.

Meanwhile the cat stretches in the slanting sun.
Meanwhile shadows climb the wall.
And still I am restless
as the night slips in.

But the moon has a certain gravity that's hard to resist.
It draws me out and I move through the yard,
gathering fallen limbs for a small fire,
a quiet apology, a pyre, I think, for the order of things.

Forgive me for not answering the phone.
I was adrift in the cosmos when you called,
my body stretched in the wild, damp clover,
my gaze fixed in the perfect spill of stars.

A Quiet Companion

Carol Anne Johnson

Anxiety knocks without warning,
slipping into the room like a draft,
cold fingers tracing the edges of thought,
whispering *what if, what if, what if.*

It builds a storm from silence,
turns footsteps into echoes,
breath into burden,
and the heart into a hurried drum.

But still—
I learn to breathe around it,
to plant my feet on steady ground,
to remind myself the present
is not as heavy as my fear suggests.

I carry small anchors:
the warmth of tea cupped in my hands,
the sound of rain against the glass,
a reminder that storms pass,
even the ones inside my chest.

Some days it rides on my shoulder,
a restless bird that won't be tamed.
Other days it grows quiet,
watching the world with me,
but not in control of my steps.

And so I keep walking,
with the weight and the light together—
learning that living with anxiety
is not about erasing the storm,
but finding my way home through the rain.

The Pool Leaks

Joshua Walker

I have a pool. It has a hole and bleeds,
but I keep pouring in water,
watching it vanish like everything else
they try to steal from me.

A tree leans over, a vine crawls its fingers in,
but I skim the surface anyway,
ritual after ritual, daring it to win.

I have a wood fence; it splintered, demanded labor,
even now it moans in the wind,
cracks gaping like open wounds—
a sieve of light they'll never patch.

I've worked my life for a pool that refuses to hold,
bled for a fence that bends and breaks.
Every day they take, claw, demand more—
but I keep the leaking water,
the warped wood, the defiance.

They try to break us, but here I sit,
cigarette burning, exposed, untamed.
The water drips, the fence groans,
and in their imperfections, I rise.

Capacities

Kerfe Roig

Just make it simple, I tell myself.
A few black lines, a white-shadowed structure.

A ladder of black lines leading into white shadows.
If there's a way down, there's a way up.

Up and down are not the only dimensions.
Infinity is full of expansive emptiness.

Emptiness can expand, saturate every illusion.
I want to become a navigator of clarity.

I want to sail on a sea of clarity without illusion.
I want to extend myself beyond artificial boundaries.

I want to discard my self-imposed boundaries.
Now or never, I think, but I've always chosen never.

As Nick Cave said, *it's late but it ain't never.*
Just make it simple, I tell myself.

Flood

Erica Johnson

It wasn't until I noticed the dog walkers returning
from the singular trail ahead of me
that I discovered there might be trouble at the turn —
a flooded path blocking any progress forward.

Cautious, I paused my walk
taking a seat upon a rock half-warmed
by the weakened winter sun which
had itself been washed out for several days.

And now I wonder is this really a problem
or an invitation to forge ahead, to bound boldly —
after all — had I not walked this trail to reconnect and
to find my way to a future less mired in grief?

And yet, while I know the flooded waters are winter cold,
I find myself removing shoes, socks, and sanity
as I stride forward into the flood — inches high:
Suck it! I shouted to the trees, but also to my tears

and washing away both my grief and fears
that had begun my day and were now flowing
off of me like the very flood I was fording across.
I am lighter for my foot bath and ready — ready for a new me!

Remembering This, You'll Laugh

Frank Johnson

It hurts to see you looking so depressed.
So depressed you looking to see it hurts.
The worst thing is I don't know what's the best.
What's the best I don't know thing is the worst
way to help put your troubled mind at rest.
At rest your troubled mind to help put way.
As you can see, I'm not a therapist,
A therapist I'm not, as you can see,
but maybe, by uttering such nonsense,
such nonsense, by uttering but maybe,
it may just coax a half smile to your lips,
to your lips a half smile just coax it may,
and then one day you'll laugh, remembering this,
and say, Thank God you're not a therapist.

Accepted

Luke Meyers

I smile
When they smile

I laugh
When they laugh

My anger rages
Silently inside

But I smile
When they smile

I laugh
When they laugh

Maybe then
I'll be accepted

At least
On the outside.

In A Silence

Paul Cannon

I love the quiet place
where the trees meet
the water and where
the stars are welcomed
as friends who speak
in a silence felt
marrow deep
as they search
my dark corners,
lessening the dull
concerns of days lost
of light and take me
once again colouring
outside the lines of
the narrow,
and out, out, beyond
to the potent throb
of life that lives in the
veins of my freedom.

It's All about Death, Really

Barbara Harris Leonhard

> *The gap between compassion and surrender is love's darkest, deepest region.*
> *—Orhan Pamuk, The Museum of Innocence*

I am ready to shed the old clothes,
the tatters that hang off my heart that I thought
held some comfort but that no longer fit me.
I lay them out for display. Touch each one,
each fear & attachment one last time.

I release my hordes of wants & needs.
My weight I put on for protection. My addictions
to coffee, chocolate, red wine.
My attraction to numbing routines,
like scrolling my way through the 'daze' as though
my time has passed.

I let go of unhealthy relationships. Minds that no longer
hold resonance to mine, may you be well.
I'll miss you, but I no longer grieve your absence
or fear abandonment.
I forgive you & myself.
I'm moving on into my vast true nature,
which holds inner wisdom & guidance
from my own tribe. I know my soul mates
will never retire.

I unburden myself from other worries. Fear of illness
& joint failure. Fear of falling.
Fear of success. Fear of defeat.
Fear of being a woman in a misogynistic world.
Fear of love & intimacy. Fear of crowds.
Fear of judgment & ridicule.
Fear of losing my mind to social dementia.

I disengage my rationalizations & projections.
They have only misled me into thinking
that I am not responsible for my pain.

Fear makes me a martyr,
felled by false beliefs.

I surrender my need to be right in any fight.
I can refract & reflect. I can move
in many directions. Not just as rays
but also waves.
Just as Soul.

I relinquish my disdain for my pesky shadow
as I know she is here to teach me,
to terrorize my naked heart
until it screams open,
and I am finally able to see
that I do not need to be 'fixed.'

My soul is no longer broken.
It's outgrown its fears.
Cleansed & ready.
Ready. For what's next.

Evenings Like This

Rachel Armes-McLaughlin

I relish in the evenings
like this, when

after a busy
and not always easy
day, we come home
and the neighborhood
kittens have come out
to play -

we go chirp at them,
then head toward our
front door, but before

we can even reach it
we smell the stew -
like a warm aura
around our home -
that we put on
hours before.

We eat.
We water our plants.

We find good fortune:

Milkweed assassin nymphs
on our pothos friend.

And I hope -

I hope, hope, hope
these memories
shape your core,
my sweet child.

Love, Ma

A Song of Flowers

Isabelle Luebke

Flower shimmering
with raindrops
and sun—

beauty has come
to this world.

Where We Let Attention Linger

Nick Allison

If I'd known what was coming
I might have stayed drunk—
wrapped in the amber hush
where edges blur
and headlines dissolve like salt.

Three years on,
thoughts scatter like pigeons
when I move too fast toward them.
If I leave them alone
they circle,
then vanish into sky.

Maybe free will is only a rumor.
Still, I can choose
which rumor to follow,
which to release
like a moth through a half-open window.

I try not to turn away
from the suffering of others,
even as the tidewaters
rise to my throat.

To reach into the clouds
without getting wet
may be impossible;
but fingertips dry quickly
in the shape of stillness,
where nothing holds,
and nothing has to.

Ladybug

Phoebe Shade

She is a splash of watercolors
dancing across the canvas of spring.

Floating like a feather
on a warm breeze,
she drifts down,
lands on my hand.

She rests,
then lets go.

Carried again by the breeze,
she finds you
and lifts one tiny wing
to wave hello—
the way ladybugs
often do.

Sleep is Negotiable

Kim Whysall-Hammond

We learnt that sleep is negotiable
but the siren wail of a newborn is not

We learnt that there is no replacement
no salve for grief, just life lived on

But that there is salvation in a gurgle
hope in a well soiled nappy

Wonder in breastfeeding
joy in Dad's skinwarmed bottle

Glory in so-soon brown eyes
in double creased fat thighs

In watching them grow
up and away

In saying goodbye
whatever the age

Survival Snacking

Meghan Woodward

Sugared tongue to cover
the bleak words, glances
enough sour candy and now
I'm numb to the walls moving
in and my heart moving out;

Salted lips savoring sadness
the cruelty, harsh reality
cuddled chip stacks snuggle
loneliness, spooning my
growing ass and dwindling will;

Chocolate dripped fingers frozen,
the destruction, brutality
darkened truffles replace
pleasure, sensation
coating me with love no longer here.

being

Melissa Lemay

maybe i've been wrong all this time
the cat lying in the pile of dirty laundry
has it all figured out

every time a monarch butterfly
flutters by, i breathe in a little magic

seeing shapes in clouds reminding
me of simpler days
why am i awake? i ask myself

the years of hurting i have mastered
i haven't ever really figured out how to live
in this skin, without any more than

dulled points and accumulated scars
pushing me down onto the floor
the names of all the things i am not

i am

i will stop wanting to fly tomorrow,
and i will breathe in all of it
the light hitting my fingertips

the sound that sinks into your heart
when you listen to my laughter
the flowerbeds, digging my fingers

into them, reaching to the other side
of the earth
this is what heaven feels like

will you come with me?

A Sprinkle of Magnetic Mist

Eileen 'ike' West

Macrocosm a mess?
I micro-dose my close community of loved ones.
Distressed for too long, I shut out the shouting, hole up,
then scribble and post old-fashioned snail-mail.
I grow calm through the writing.
Others, too—I'm told—in the reading.

Dear friends, I'm finally unpacking
the last boxes and bags,
Planting a flag on the mountainside,
I mark entry to my new home in the forest.
Now, a day's ride from any big city,
I'm give-or-take an hour east of the Pacific.
Ultimately, Maestro Weather orchestrates
the length of drive time to anywhere.

Open an envelope, expose a handwritten letter—
it's rare and well-anticipated.
Finding words to splash on the page
only starts our pulling together.
Sure, amidst the havoc of daily living,
I extract things worth recall and respect.
But the real work
(not corralling my thoughts)
grows in communal mind space.

For the unfamiliar, let me share a glimpse
of Oregon's winter weather:
Bleak, bitter, finger-frosting cold,
churned out of heavy leaden peasoupers.
Weather aces claim one singular culprit
causes our frigid gloom—
the dastardly malefactor is…the Gulf of…

Ok, ok. Here's an aside:
I moseyed on over here from Texas
where I absorbed a knee-jerk mental 'fact'—
mi compadres, the Gulf is MEXICAN.
But here, in O-R, weather blusters about,
throwing itself south from the Gulf of…

Wait for it,
while my Texas mind switches gears
to the foreign Gulf of ALASKA.

In writing, I highlight humor,
if only a smidgeon,
that speaks to the wildness within,
Helps us remain whole
in a culture that instructs us
to never mind that.
Not anymore.
Still, I toss away weighty matters
and instead glitzify co-habitating
with the elements.
Despite the macrocosmic agenda
to snuff it out,
I pledge allegiance to normalcy.

This week, the OR coast
flips its weatherly switch.
The origins, no gulf,
but rather, paradise.
Tempests bolt across P. Ocean,
while Ms Misty Troposphere,
fiendishly thirsty,
sucks up water and bliss-bombs us
with warm, overgenerous splatters
from southern-most Hawaii.
Yup. Alaska, Hawaii and Oregon
make a trio of states united climatically.

My stories—some scream,
others whisper—
all arise motley and multilayered.
Personal myths made solid,
bricked with fears, doubts, dreams,
and courage.
Once mailed, tendrils of healing
and renewal sprout across USPS-land.
At this, something inside me
perks to life.
Bull's eye!
Instantly, creativity bests turmoil.

Today, walking through the rain,
and not shivering,
I reach out with open palms,
Tickled by the earthbound
plop, plop, plops.
I laugh, pretending each wet missive
arrives special delivery
to me from Hawaii.
And now sitting on my porch
writing you,
A soft wind touches my face.
Certain it carries
the faint strumming of a ukelele,
I smile.

My marks on the page
give people no answers,
offer no certainties
in the sharing.
What arrives in the mail
proves little more
than a magnetic mist,
a momentary center of attention,
a distraction aimed
at the drawing out
from precious minds
imaginative delights
that clear debris
and inspire joy.

No matter if our winds
blow from north,
or south,
or follow a whirl of routes,
Going forward,
let's hope we're all showered
with blessings—tender drops—
Some big like mountains,
others just tiny sprinkles.
Maybe even a few
garnished with exotic
island melodies.

Black Moments

Nicole Sara

Black moments bite, they take their share
and leave a sorrowful mark
Black moments burn, feeding on air,
with flames shaping the dark

Black moments blow like fierce winds moaning,
unleashing ice through the days…
Black moments beat an unyielding tempo
stifling the magical rays

Black moments breathe through smiles and light,
turning our eyes from the sun
Black moments breaking free from the fetters,
transforming nights into white

Black moments beg to be painted sweet blue,
green or yellow or pink…
Black moments bending the time and the skies,
spewing an eerie ink

For black moments bathe the wonderful air
in mantles and curtains of night
becoming the bridge for the cold deep sighs
towards bright beautiful flight

Heavy

R.M. Carlson

lead in my belly
lead in my heart
I sit
in thoughts of you

realize
I'm afraid
of reaching out
to you

afraid your words
will bring shame
like a cloud
settling over me

did you cheer them on?
with their flags and guns?
did you laugh
at those forced to hide?

or did shame humble you
disgust you
bring you back to reality
by their sedition?

if I reach out
talk with you
what will you say?
who are you now?

I sit heavy
with foreboding
my dread skittering
like insects
in my belly

who are you?

Life Sentence

Frank Johnson

Life's to be lived so live for today
or carpe diem if your Latin's OK
and don't lose the will to live or say
life ain't worth living coz you only live once
and life's too short, as we're here today
gone tomorrow and from cradle to grave
ain't that long a stay and life is a cabaret,
old chum, the best things in life are free,
living is easy with eyes closed
and life's not about how many breaths you take
but the moments that take your breath away
so live and let live, eat, drink and be merry
and let tomorrow look after itself,
our little life being rounded with a sleep,
and life, what is it but a dream
which is not to say life can't be cruel
as nothing is certain but death and taxes
and tomorrow and tomorrow and tomorrow
and all our yesterdays
are not today, thank you,
so look lively coz he came to save the living
not the dead, and live as if every day was your last
although it's not a matter of life or death
(it's more important than that) and
remembering God writes straight on crooked lives
live life to the full
stop

Alone at Night

Sam Hendrian

I'm good at being alone
Except after 6 PM
When the sun abandons me
And the moon hides its picky eyes.

Suddenly it seems like a crime
Not to be with someone,
Not to be held tight
During the darkest parts of the night.

Too early to escape into dreams
So I manufacture dreams of my own
With the aid of rock star medication,
The kind that strengthens then poisons.

Then in the morning I shake my head
Wondering how I expect to get ahead
If I keep deflecting temporary endless pain
Through endless temporary pleasure.

But once evening returns to its post
I remember every logically illogical excuse
For perpetrating vacant charms
'Til I'm resting in somebody's arms.

Friends

Kerfe Roig

1

Friends arrive in random order,
not really invited, yet braiding
themselves into your being until
they become knots that keep
the chaos from fraying your edges—
you reflect and are reflected,
an embellished outline containing
universes that the rest of the world
unsees—all that is your otherness
becomes connected as you bear
witness to each other's lives

2

A friend is a river upon which
you can float when you are
too tired of swimming, a vessel
to hold your grief when you feel
overwhelmed by circumstances—
when all your paths are blocked
by walls and your skies sit heavy
and grey, a friend opens the door
and gives you space, becomes
a mirror that shows not your faults
but a way around your obstacles

3

A friend is a light in the dark—
no cliché ever held more truth

I think we should have some make-believe

Erica Johnson

Frankly, I welcomed the book
as it took me and the sleepy
blanket far from the humdrum town.

Together we crunched on tacos,
before peeling back the skin
of a peach with our precarious pens.

How were we to know
that all we would find along the way
was a pack of stickers and
a twirly yellow bubble wand
"pause and pop" it sang to our delight!

Each bubble burst released
a fuzzy, buzzy bumblebee —
scattering across the sky
like champagne starlight.

We drank that sweet honey-nectar
till we grew wings of our own.

Giggling wind chimes — blanket, book, and I
tumbled down into the tickle-me-pink tulips
and wrapped ourselves together
in the woolly warmth of Mr. Rogers' scarlet cardigan:
Did you know it's alright to wonder?

Anthem of the Leaking Roof

Joshua Walker

Storm after storm,
I place buckets under the drips.
The ceiling peels, the floor stains,
but still—I catch the rain.

Some nights I dance in the leak,
bare feet slapping water,
like I'm mocking the sky itself:
is this all you've got?

The roof will cave someday—
fine.
Until then, my buckets are thrones,
and I sit crowned by persistence.

After the Breaking

Carol Anne Johnson

The silence after storm
is never clean—
it hums with echoes,
splinters of a voice
you did not choose.

You walk through it barefoot,
collecting pieces,
sometimes cutting yourself
on memories that refuse
to dull.

But healing does not ask for haste.
It is the small, stubborn act
of opening curtains to light,
of naming the hurt aloud,
of breathing despite the heaviness
pressing on your chest.

You are not what was done to you.
You are the pulse that survived it,
the trembling hand
that still reaches
for warmth.

And though the shadows
still curl at your feet,
your steps—
slow, uneven,
unapologetically your own—
are teaching the ground
how to hold you again.

Falling, Flying

Merril D. Smith

Leaves, rain, night,
a bullet-ripped child—

so many things fall,
are falling—

the crows, black-winged tocsins,
sound warnings,

but it's
the geese I observe—

the parents still guarding
their almost-grown goslings,

the way they listen for the call to fly
then take turns leading.

I watch them soar,
hear the wind-flap of their wings—

I'm not starving, nor beaten,
nor bombed; I'm not a child raped
then cowed into silence. I have not yet
been coerced or suppressed—though it may come—

today, I imagine
flying with the geese

through grey clouds and brilliant blue sky,
swift-shifting in surf-spray
whiffling and sideslipping,
like autumn leaves, twirling
almost upside-down

before landing just right.

Triage

Audrey Howitt

I tape over my cracked edges.
The memories
the smells
the wanting
what I can't have. There is always that.
A hole I can't fill
that pulls those edges apart.
And every day, I sit in it
let it unfold me, just under the skin
until the angles need mending again.
I tell them it will be ok,
that they will see the sun
the sky
the water
even when the wind blows me open
against my outer walls.
It is who I am right now.
All I know is this widening chasm
and the hope that the tape in this tiny drawer
will be enough.

Fear

Kim Whysall-Hammond

Bury it deep, weep
if you need. Plead with yourself. Else
you lose your mind.

Discover what you can do. You
are a fluttering bird, who once flew.

Take joy in a friend, end your despair, air
your burdened soul. Roll
with the glorious world.

Unfurl.

Grounded

Paul Cannon

When the insistent
dull roar of the
world reaches
murderous crescendo
in my body,
its long knives piercing,
I take my wounded self
along bush paths
folding into nature,
just for my soul,
spice under my tongue,
I hear the musicality,
see the intricate
brush strokes, feel
every sheaf of poetry
that flutters or
rustles nearby,
and slowly I
come back into
my body.

Mirror Pantoum

Kate Bremer

I took down the sparkle-lines--
Severe drought, Red Flag warnings
For two trees, for Faeries, for Light;
Fill up water bottles and charge devices.

Severe drought, Red Flag conditions--
Jacob's Well has dried up.
Fill water bottles and charge devices
Where's the manna, the talking cloud ?

Jacob's Well has dried up
For two trees, for Faeries, for Light--
Where's the manna, the talking cloud ?
I took down the sparkle-lines tonight.

The Cartography of Quiet

Brent Boeckman

Standing in the shrapnel of a former world,
despite the constant shore, failing and falling away.
The call, heavy, carrying the dull, metallic scent
of a fierce fight lost—
the quiet ruin when every effort is given,
yet the whole thing collapses.

Underneath the chaos, the governing law revealed:
a silent, binding contract signed decades ago,
mandating the role as always secondary.
Articulating this prime directive, a hush falling on deaf ears.
The mechanism seizing. Seeing the blueprint of life's choices—
a script written by others, for one to perform.

Confessing of spiritual-death to an internal vacancy,
the clocks only measuring obligation, never zest.
One's own sustenance perpetually last on the ledger.
A sorrowful tone running low, but beneath it,
a faint electricity: the refusal to flee.
A willingness to turn the gaze *inward* for once,
facing the source, not just the symptom.

Resolve creates beginning, beginning takes shape.
Defining the atmospheric pressure lived under—
the ceaseless, exhausting oscillation.
One hour, a pillar, firmly anchored;
the next, a compass needle spinning, lost and untethered.
The brutal rhythm of strength chased by surrender.

A door opens—not to destruction, but to air.
Finding a simple, deep-seated rest unknown since youth.
Alone, the need to present a certain image vanishes.
The quiet and absolute lack of noise is healing.
The simple awareness that peace is the residue of not being
constantly needed—
but becoming the very first, stable platform for the rebuild.

In Between

Frank Johnson

Now everybody's staring at a screen
it seems a simple fact of modern life
that real life's left for living in between.

Sometimes despite the wonders of IT
it looks less of a blessing than a blight
when everybody's staring at a screen

for world-wide web can all too easily mean
there's world-wide room for wrong as well as right,
real life being left for living in between.

And please don't think IT will set you free:
you work for Mark, Jeff, Elon and their like,
now everybody's staring at a screen.

So pull the plug, relax, stroll by a stream,
stop staring, be a latter-day Luddite.
Don't leave your life for living in between.

And before you accuse me of hypocrisy,
it's just that I'm an online type of writer
who cannot but be staring at a screen
with real life left for living in between.

naked

Melissa Lemay

it's been three weeks
i still haven't changed the sheets on my bed,
i've barely changed my clothes

i wonder what was real,
if i'm real,
sitting in this apartment with this fake wood flooring

and the linoleum tile with the diamonds on it
i listen to the sound of water dripping
everything was wet

i know my bedroom is down the hall
i've begun making a habit of only sleeping in it
i work in the living room

bedrooms are for sleeping
there isn't any place inside you haven't been
helping me fold my laundry

putting together bunk beds
outside, playing football with the kids
you were at the birthday party filming everything

i can't smell you anywhere, anymore
i wonder if your dreams are sweet
i love you more

Paradise is

Nicole Sara

What is a promise, a dream?
What is a hope or desire?
What is a heart's burning flame
setting all senses
on fire?

What is the mind's
adventure
and which is the soul's sweet ease?
What if the life's sole purpose
is being caressed by

the breeze…

Do days always reach for remoteness
and dawns always shine so divine
casting far chime over moments,
driving refrain and
new rhyme?

When frowns or smiles,
or doubts
orbit each minute's deep beats,
deeper yet heavenly rays
pierce from across

bluer seas…

Longing for further,
for warmer
yearning for promising skies,
golden triumphant tomorrows
beyond strained sinews
and eyes

Ploughing and steering steadily
ready to fall to your knees,
holding horizons at heart
finding what

paradise is...

Embroidery

Kerfe Roig

She was weary of her fragile subsistence, of the looming and inevitable collapse of any scaffolding of support. The gatekeepers distributed no methods of survival, only rampant indifference. Despair mingled with neglect. She floated on swirling waters that never seemed to drift towards any shore. Her solitude ached like a dark tunnel too small to hold even the palest of light.

Each day became an impossible pilgrimage through the immensity of her hunger, her grief. Where was she going? She did not know.

in the beginning
empty hands—gathering, then
listening, feeling

Her hands became entwined with the rhythms of the circles she had traveled, over and over, spinning the earth's gifts into fibers that shimmered with their own light. She passed them through the portal of the needle, the intersected web of fabric, in, out, over, under, through.

thread transformed--
trees, birds, landscape, sky—
sanctuary

The Ashtray Teaches Me Discipline

Joshua Walker

I stub out one more cigarette,
line it among the others like a row of soldiers—
burned, blackened, but still proof
that I stood here, breathing smoke instead of silence.

The world keeps breaking windows,
keeps hammering nails into my wrists,
but I light, I drag, I exhale,
and in that small cloud I build a barricade.

They call it weakness—
I call it ritual.
Even poison can become a prayer
if it keeps your hands from shaking.

Sailing advice for survival and tales of disgust from across the Atlantic Rift

Sue McBean

Ice cold breasts.
Misled by September sun,
chilled at sea.
Don protective layers
at earliest perception of cold.

From first sail I sensed
Mankind has always been at sea.
I feel no fear,
except performing Man Overboard drill.
Alone.

We edge forward
at pace of fast walking.
Five knots from wind.
Lifted another knot from tide behind.
Blind except for sky messages,
senses,
instrument information,
held by testimony of trusted commentators,
mappers and historians.

Planning based on
experience of years,
and lore of forefathers:
set against chaos,
and powerful tidal races.

Preparedness because
a boat cannot be parked,
only tied to earth or anchor.
Think ahead.
Tide strength, times, direction and
useful eddies.
Berth before the small craft warning unfolds.
Visibility. Sea state.

Positioning signal: to see and be seen.
Thick socks bearing letters L and R
and best sailing boots.

Seamless team.
No criticism to avoid distraction.
Rituals. Focus. Cross check.
To prevent sinking: Bolt the bulkhead,
secure the Fastnet washboards
and seal the anchor locker.

Heeled over. Sounds of crockery tumbling
and book flying.
Essential the cabin is hazard-free underway.
Careless stowing created
fall risk during inspection.
Descend companionway steps,
against roller coaster forces,
all four limbs gripping,
climbing with no harness.

The first time the cat sailed, her litter was placed,
on a floor space under our night quarters.
Stench in the night.
She searches for flies, eyes cormorants,
considers playing with waves. No fear
of dangers we see. We watch
lest she jumps when she should shelter.

Buds banned from ear use
dried the canal after showering.
Sound as rasp of metal file, and
loud squelch as boot sucking out of a deep bog.
Astonishing sight withdrawn.
Insect encased in amber wax,
antennae pointing.
Each night unbearable itch,
from what is left behind.

Fraudulent conifer played doorstep dwarf
for a decade. Released to soil,
villain qualities emerged by stealth.
Cut off it harms no more.

Beneath the music
Prufrock heard the dying fall of voices.
But there was no music.
Only bullets killing
children in a sanctuary, people in their home.

Where wild forget-me-nots bloomed yesterday,
last night a thug pulled them up.
He didn't know.
They've already seeded.

We comfort each other at night.
Guarding against intruders
and foulness where it shouldn't be.

We are Not the Same

Rachel Armes-McLaughlin

You drop bombs
tearing across sky
black bird of prey -

I drop words
on page.

I march,
I demonstrate.

Yet we hail from
same coordinates,

Whiteman
Air Base -

My father controlled
your airspace,
controlled

you.

He is gone, but his
zeal for violence
still reigns
on the base
where I was birthed.

This poem was written in response to the June 22, 2025 bombing of Iran, which was carried out by B-2 stealth bombers originating from Whiteman Air Force Base in Missouri, where the aircrafts are stationed and where the author was born.

Wanting

Aubrey Phoenix

Sometimes I am aware of our societal programming.
I resist the mundane dance of living to work—
Far too often, I feel the worm in my head
influencing me
to spend,
to consume,
to want—
always wanting
to have someone,
to hold something,
to be someone.

Society is designed
to make us want
and to always feel like
we can never have enough,
we can never be satiated
with the faux comfort
of living the "dream" we bought without question.

The wanting is built in.
If we can never make enough money to survive,
how are we supposed to stop buying—
to feel satisfied?

Sometimes the only solace in this capitalist hellscape
seems to be an $8 coffee and a breakfast burrito,
or maybe something we think makes us more special—
authentic—
maybe something that means nothing,
but provides a nice boost of serotonin
and pads our shelves and walls,
creating some false sense of security.

This is all we know how to do.
It's what we've been taught:
"Everyone does it."

If you're not wanting,
you must be doing it wrong.
There's always the next big thing,
another corporate ladder to climb,
a fad diet to lose weight,
a family member to gain approval from.
It never ends.

I'm learning that this wanting
is programmed into us
not to genuinely improve our lives
but to improve the lives of others.

The more we buy,
the more money we give to giant corporations;
the more we strive to move up,
the more of our lives we give to The Man;
the more time we spend focused on losing weight,
the less we love and accept ourselves—
the less we buy their products.

Wanting is a losing battle.
No matter how much you
buy, move up, or change for others,
you will never be satisfied.

There is always something more expensive
mocking you from the store shelf.
There is always someone above you making more money,
refusing to retire.
There is always someone
with a slimmer waist receiving more patriarchal approval.

What do I catch myself doing in my free time?
Scrolling through online stores and Facebook Marketplace,
through endless aisles of people who are "happier,"
"healthier," "wealthier,"
mocking us through blue-lit screens.

We're searching hopelessly for something without a name,
because it's undefinable.
Because it's unattainable.

I want happiness—
well, what is happiness?
Being stable and successful.
Well, what does that mean?
Being able to afford where I live,
and work a job that brings me joy
while spending time with people that I love.

Does any of that sound like consumerism to you?

Shaken

R.M. Carlson

lost my faith
my anchor
my purpose
broken
soul stripped bare
aching, grieving
exposed, raw

separated from
hypocrisy
unchained
from that
which I do not believe

just a little pride
peeks through
shoulders back
chin up
time to be me

I am righteous anger
seeking justice
don't look away
bear witness

children starving
ribs exposed
some kind of twisted
target practice

masked men
unmarked cars
families taken
in the night

homeless removed
nowhere to go
unhoused? a crime
now go to jail

I am love
embrace
the awkward
the shunned
the scapegoats
the hurting
the poor
I care

I am peace
in nature
birds early and late
create melodies
winds sough
branches sway
inchworm inches
reaching, contracting

heart at rest
opening, seeking
I am not broken;
I have broken free
What is belief?
I believe in me

On Disappearing

Audrey Howitt

I watch footage when it's available.
White men in masks take you, and you go.
What else can you do in a country
where you thought you could speak out?

If I could,
I would form keys from the fingers of your captors,
I would cry on the spot they took you,
I would pin your image, your name, your breath
to any place, any person who can keep you safe.

You didn't bargain for this.
None of us did.

Your mothers
fathers
sisters
brothers
nieces
nephews, so like mine,
call out your name to the wind,
ask God, Allah, Mohamed, anyone, everyone
to keep you safe
from those who would erase you.

You have landed in the maw
without knowing it.

I would take your hand,
lead you home to the hearts
that hold you before it is too late.

For you.
For all of us.

Our Lady, the Future

Kim Whysall-Hammond

We are a gate by which she enters
we accidental gods
we must dance as fast as we can

Fear cannot not take hold of us
we must be furious
hold fast to life, to laughter
to the birdsong that lifts our Sun
to rain that waters and cleanses
to clear streams and bright skies

She is the ghost of things to come
no more black water
no poisons
no hatred
children free of hunger, war and fear

She will set us all free, she is life's flood

Oh, won't it be glorious
life resurgent, victorious
we can lie down with the lion and the lamb
clasp hands and paws together
hear the elephants call to victory
the moment is coming

Prepare to love
and finally
to live.

After Rob Green, UK songwriter and positive genius.

Another Two Dollars

Sam Hendrian

At sunset on Sunset Boulevard
When West Hollywood was waking up
An aspiring actress of 25
Limped back to her studio apartment.

Didn't know she was poor
'Til she dropped her toothbrush on the ground
And cursed in fear
Of having to lose another two dollars.

Ten days into sobriety so far
Which would have been an accomplishment
If it hadn't been January
The month of false resolutions.

Longed to be held
But not held accountable
Which limited her partners
To one-night knights.

A vibrator used to work wonders
Before her springtime imagination
Broke between May and December
Trying to shield a fading dream.

Now pleasure and sorrow were equals
Daily happy hour specials
That kept her alive
Yet unable to thrive.

Hartford Meadow

Edward St. James

The nerves have long stretched outwards from my spine
Sudden noises and piles of paperwork stretching above
All while fascism grows and nightmares stand in a line
I dream of becoming a dove in a grove

Sudden noises and piles of paperwork stretching above
Only daydreams can keep me moving forward
I dream of becoming a dove in a grove
Of all the songs that are played by bearded bards

Only daydreams can keep me moving forward
When all the buildings stretch out into shadow
Of all the songs that are played by bearded bards
My favorite is the tragic one about Hartford Meadow

When all the buildings stretch into shadow
I alone with my pen and my humming do sing
My favorite is the tragic one about Hartford Meadow
I hope you don't mind if we clap while we wing

I alone with my pen and my humming do sing
All while fascism grows and nightmares stand in a line
I hope you don't mind if we clap while we wing
The nerves have long stretched outwards from my spine

Writing with the Herd

Kate Bremer

Tucker greets us today—messenger from other worlds;
He travels back and forth so easily in the quiet, between
the trees, under the shrill of Bodi's squeaky toy.
Something is happening!

Donkey squeals! Pony runs! Sylvia runs! The world is speeding
up again. Time to slow the pen. Neutron star,
heavier than Jasper, Marshmallow and all our drums. Marshmallow
wants to play all the instruments, eat all the notebooks, make poetry.

I feel your soft beautiful breath; Today we're inhaled by horses.
Thank you for lungs, bird wings stirring the air, sage clearing
our bodies, leaf sounds, bare feet, large nostrils, gentle lips.
Distracted by animal neurons, folds of grief, hearts unraveling—
For some reason the birds start to sing;
Feral cat jumps from the wood pile.

Bird

Zsófia Hajnal

Bird in a cage
You want to be free
Imagine the world more beautiful
Than it could
Ever be

And so
The idea of wonder
Is born
And sung in an age
Of captivity

A Protest Piece

Erica Johnson

I decided to partake
popping over to a protest
and demonstrating democracy
I was not prepared for
a capital crisis on the capitol
where the lines are drawn
not unlike the lines we drew
in permanent marker on poster
which warbles with movement
and the din of voices
ebbing, flowing, weaving
around and into the streets
arms linked or outstretched
and stomping feet standing
or sitting stamping
and always
call and response
call and response
TAKE ACTION and
chanting, chanting, chanting
color bleeds across concrete
leading up to steps
United We Stand!

employed

Melissa Lemay

i hold the plunger
between my teeth
and

pull
it
back.

draw-
ing
the liquid into the
barrel. it is the color
of a camel.

i find the pool-blue
marker in the
crook of my elbow.

piercing my skin, a
dark-dance oblivion
follows after red.

i wake up, unsure
of when; where
begins to come into
focus.

i am late to work
again.

The Quiet Landing

Brent Boeckman

Standing in the rubble of a life split wide open.
Not a door ajar, but the whole damn house blown in.
The discovery of a person who poured every drop
of cement into the crack—
watching the foundation still just… snap.

The raw mix: Exhaustion. Confusion.
The voice thick with the simple, brutal intrusion of failure,
even when doing everything right, yet feeling so "dead inside."
Living from duty. Not desire.
A steady, grey tide, prioritizing everyone else, always, over the self.
Where one's own soul quietly knelt.

Grief as the undertone, the audible thrum, but beneath it,
a faint hum—a low, ready chord.
A willingness to look inward.
To finally stop running from the pain that had been coming,
and coming.
"The fog," the brutal, constant split.
One moment: Powerful. Grounded. A fortress wall.
The next: Miserable. Disoriented. Ready to fall.
The brutal swing between the collapse and the strength.
The fight fought a whole life's length.

But beneath the ground, the old reflex seated—
a script, etched deep, where the choice is always flat:

"My whole existence has been everybody else's priority over me."

Stating it. Then, stopping.
The world pausing.
The pendulum dropping.
Something landing.
The recognition. The invisible script. The old, worn-out condition.
A crack opening—not the violent kind this time.

A quiet door to a peace that isn't a crime.

Songs of Morning

Nick Allison

When I awoke today,
I looked to the east
and there was the sun,
punctual as ever.

I opened the back door,
pleased to hear the birds
singing their songs of morning
into the cool, quiet air.

Breathing in, I feel my lungs
expand, contract. Steady,
the beat of my heart,
a small promise of existence.

The world goes on as it does,
unburdened by the weight of our fears,
chirps the chickadee
from her perch in the cedar elm,
high above it all.

Here Now

Rachel Armes-McLaughlin

I wore my favorite shoes,
rubber-soled, out in the rain
to keep me grounded on the Earth.

Black canvas tops,
white laces -
covering my warm feet,
feet walking down
the asphalt hill
at twilight.

Cold, cold rain -
late winter,
early spring.

The heavy waste bag
keeps me weighted,
fingers numbing
from the looped strings,
arm tired, and my shoes
grounding me in the rain.

Suddenly:
wet canvas, cold toes.

Water rushes, ripples
down the blacktop,
spreads,
covering my feet.

All I feel is cold,
here and now.

Moments later, walking home
from the dump bin,
umbrella is blown by a gust
and I feel more weightless,

vision blurred
by foggy, rain-spattered glasses.

And as I walk,
the sound of my soaked
but grounded feet:

Here now,
here now,
here now....

The Last Forever

Nicole Sara

I forgive winters their harsh silences,
their inexistent arrivals
timidly scattered
on the winding pathways
within me...
I step along your mild quietness
in every sigh
treading carefully on your shadows
    among time drops always the same…

You always open the door,
and then a window
for my flight
not begun yet...
And I rewrite the same verse
from the abyss
always lost and found
in your eyes
    when you rekindle the stars…

I sprinkle white petals of togetherness
all along the labyrinth humming deep echoes
and slowly
fading away in the mists...
Where you lost my way
not entwining your dream
    with mine

...but fragrantly leaving behind
the warmest
and always the last
forever

Now When We Are Living in a Darkening World

Merril D. Smith

I want to taste every season on
my tongue—

spring lilacs, summer roses,
autumn's dried brown leaves
as they crunch underfoot,
winter snow,
the scent of it
about to fall—

I want to see stars in my eyes
and notice the spaces   in between

like the pause   when it seems the sky

is holding a breath just before the storm.

I want to remember that
feathered hope can fly
through black holes
and beyond space and time

into sighs of susurrus
or prickles of petrichor

where I can swallow it—

hope is the scent of brewed coffee,
the most delicious chocolate,
a strawberry freshly picked, sun-warmed
and ripe.

It is every baby's laugh.

Carrying the Invisible

Carol Anne Johnson

Each morning, the weight is waiting,
quiet as stone beneath the chest.
I lace my shoes and breathe through the fog,
a soldier rehearsing peace.

The world asks for smiles like currency,
but mine are stitched from fragile threads.
Behind them, a storm hums low and constant,
lightning without thunder.

Still, I move.
Step by step,
cup of tea in hand,
pill bottles like lighthouses lining the shore.

Some days, I speak gently to myself—
as if I were a child learning to walk again.
Other days, I let silence cradle me,
knowing rest can be resistance too.

There are small victories no one sees:
leaving bed when gravity says stay,
answering a message instead of folding inward,
finding laughter that feels like air after drowning.

This is not weakness.
It is survival in its rawest form—
an art of carrying the invisible
while still reaching for the light.

And though the illness lingers,
so do I.

"It may be that when we no longer know what to do,
we have come to our real work."

—Wendell Berry

Contributor Bios

Meridith Allison lives on the edge of the Gila Wilderness in southwestern New Mexico with her family. She writes often, finishes pieces occasionally, and shares her work rarely—usually only when her brother, who happens to be an editor on this project, insists. She's very fond of walking and of her little dog, Boo.

Nick Allison is a writer and editor based in Austin, Texas. You can find more of his work at TheTruthAboutTigers.com.

Rachel Armes-McLaughlin has written poetry for nearly 25 years. Her work is published in *The Chaos Section Poetry Project*, where she currently assists as co-editor; in venues such as Loblolly Press, Middle Mouse Press, and *Medicine and Meaning*; in a Central Arkansas Library System anthology; and elsewhere, with one poem nominated for Best of the Net and another nominated for a 2025 Pushcart Prize. Rachel lives in the very red state of Arkansas with her husband, Jack; daughter, Isabelle; and four cats. You can find her on BlueSky at @mother-poet.bsky.social.

Brent Boeckman is a men's somatic trauma and emotional resiliency coach and has been writing poetry as a means of expression, healing, and connection for as long as he can remember. He leads with his heart, is a proud father, and is a community advocate for mental health.

Kate Bremer loves to write in nature with friends, donkeys, birds, and horses. She lives on a small farm near Blanco, TX.

Paul Cannon is a poet who contemplates the mysteries of life in all its wonder and his experiences of the journey. Paul lives with his wife Lyn in the south-west corner of Australia where two oceans meet, a place that inspires life and writing.

With a B.S. in Communications, **R.M. Carlson's** career over the years has covered marketing, public relations, and scientific and research journal management and publishing. As a child, she wrote and illustrated stories and has continued to write as a hobby ever since. Her focus shifted to poetry after taking a college poetry class. Her strong sense of social justice was established early in life by the ideals of her working-class parents, who actively engaged in politics, community, and more. She was raised in a church with progressive values that actively fought for social justice in and outside the local area. R.M. Carlson seeks ways she can make a difference, however small, in the world. Poetry has become her middle finger extended toward fascism.

Bonner Fowles is an Austin-born artist based in Central Texas. He works with multiple mediums, with a strong focus on drawing and both oil and acrylic painting.
bonnerfowles-artist-austintx.yolasite.com

Zsófia Hajnal is a Budapest-based Hungarian economist and poet. In 2024, while her doctoral dissertation *Reinterpreting the Moral Economy*, written at the Corvinus University of Budapest, approached its final stages, a selection of her poems titled *Unfulfilled* was published as well. She is a contributor to the upcoming anthology *My Sweet Mother*. Zsófia lived five years of her childhood in Germany and studied for several months at a UK university as a young adult. She began writing poems and anecdotes in the late 2010s. What she enjoys about writing—beyond self-expression and the recharging function of the process—are the frequent coincidences, mostly in the form of rhymes that arise in the lines as if by external design. Zsófia is a regular reader at the open mic events of the Budapest Poetry Collective.

Barbara Harris Leonhard writes from her soul's longing. She fills her pen with grief, joy, satire, sorrow, and story. She is the editor for *MasticadoresUSA* and *FEED THE HOLY*. You can follow her at ExtraordinarySunshineWeaver.blog.

Sam Hendrian is a Los Angeles-based filmmaker, poet, and playwright striving to foster empathy through art. From writing personalized poems for passersby outside of LA's oldest independent bookstore every Sunday to making Chaplin-esque silent films about loneliness and human connection once a month, Sam lives to make other people feel seen and validated. More poems and films can be found on Instagram at @samhendrian143.

Audrey Howitt lives and writes poetry in the San Francisco Bay Area. When not writing, she sings opera and teaches voice. She is also a licensed attorney and a licensed marriage and family therapist. Ms. Howitt has been published in *Academy of the Heart and Mind, Washington Square Review, Panoply, Hecate Magazine, Spillwords Press, Nymphs Poetry Journal, Muddy River Poetry Review, The Big Windows Review, The White Cresset Arts Journal, Total Eclipse Poetry and Prose, Chiaroscuro—Darkness and Light, dVerse Poets Anthology, With Painted Words, Algebra of Owls,* and *Lost Towers Publications.*

Carol Anne Johnson is a 45-year-old blind woman living in Ireland. She is a child abuse survivor, diagnosed with complex PTSD and dissociative identity disorder. She writes as a form of therapy, which helps her cope. She loves reading, volunteering, and writing.

Erica Johnson has spent her entire life navigating the different spaces of central Arkansas: from graduating out of the crowded halls of Mills University Studies High School to teaching in the much more rural Vilonia High School. Erica is a regular poet in online spaces such as *EthicalELA* and *Teach Write.* She spends her non-writing time taking in various anime and learning new games.

Frank Johnson lives in Coventry, England. In addition to poetry, his interests include painting and learning Irish. More of his poetry can be found at ashortspell.com/francopomes-2
Career: postman; postal and telegraph officer; registrar of births, deaths and marriages; polytechnic/university administrator; interpreter and translator (from Czech and Portuguese); retired. Poetry publications: 2013: *Boscombe Revolution*; 2023: AUB International Poetry Competition, highly commended; Erbacce Press, ten poems, highly commended; 2024: *Frogmore Papers, Swerve*; 2025: *Locofo Anti-Trump Anthology: Poems for Freedom*; *Wildfire Words*; Waltham Forest Poetry Competition: 1st Prize for funny poem.

Melissa Lemay lives in Lancaster County, Pennsylvania, with her children and cats. She writes about God, addiction, trauma, healing, motherhood, and many other things. She enjoys spending time with family, drinking good coffee, and being outdoors. She loves animals. Her poem "Ephemeral" was chosen as Poetic Publication of the Year for 2023 at *Spillwords Press*; she was Author of the Month for July 2024 and Author of the Year for 2024. Find her at melissalemay.wordpress.com, collaborature.blogspot.com, and at dVerse Poets Pub.

Nine-year-old **Isabelle Luebke** lives in Little Rock, Arkansas and spends time equally with her dad, Brandon Luebke, and her mom, Rachel Armes-McLaughlin, who is co-editor on this book. Isabelle likes to draw, play with her many cats and dogs (and one fish), help her mom with poetry, play Pokemon video games with her dad, and spend special time with her bonus parents, Danielle and Jack. Her favorite animals are cats, especially her cats - Luna, Max, Ripley, Phantom, Wednesday, Mera, and Miette.

Sue McBean is a sailor, nurse teacher, wildflower photographer, and botanist who writes creatively. Living for many years now on the north coast of Northern Ireland, she was brought up on the flat lands of the Cambridgeshire Fens. Sue writes mainly prose with a poetic style, reflecting on her life and exploring themes of sea, sailing, island life, and nature. She is interested in overlaying difficult experiences with beauty, art, and laughter, and is currently writing a memoir, a series of essays about well-being, and children's stories. Sue felt most honoured to have a poem published earlier this year by *The Chaos Section Poetry Project* in *Record of Dissent: Poems of Protest in an Authoritarian Age*.

Luke Meyers is a Welsh writer and poet who started writing during lockdown. He has been published in anthologies by *Icebreakers Lit*, *From One Line*, and *Muse Pie Press*, as well as writing on Bluesky at @sonnetsmith.bsky.social.

Aubrey Phoenix is a twenty-six-year-old nonbinary, neurodivergent, alternative artist struggling to survive in America—but surely not the only one. Raised in a self-help, toxically positive "it's all in your head if you get sick" household, they hastened away from adolescence into adulthood, naively trusting that the world would welcome them on a path to their destined success. Their rose-tinted glasses shattered when their existence and truth proved time and time again to be something they would have to fight for. Their first book, *All The Things I Left Unfinished*, shares poems from some of their rawest moments of self-discovery—harrowing accounts of parental trauma, heartbreak, and struggles with bipolar II disorder in early adulthood. You can find more of Aubrey's work on their website, aubreyphoenix.com

A resident of New York City, **Kerfe Roig** enjoys transforming words and images into something new. Her poetry and art have been featured online by *Silver Birch Press, Feral, Pure Haiku, Zen Space, Visual Verse, Collaborature,* and *The Ekphrastic Review,* and published in *Ella@100, Incandescent Mind, The Raw Art Review, The Anthropocene Hymnal,* and *The Polaris Trilogy.* Follow her explorations on her blogs, methodtwomadness.wordpress.com (which she does with her friend Nina) and kblog.blog.

Nicole Sara is a bilingual poet from Romania, with a master's degree in Philology and American Studies from the "Al. I. Cuza" University in Iași. She loves languages and performing magic with words. Nicole began by writing poems in Romanian, and in 2016 she started pairing the originals with their translation into English. She finds inspiration in the beauty and intelligence of everything around her. *Rhyming Dreams,* Nicole's debut collection of poems and original photographs, was self-published on Amazon in 2024, and she has recently published her second collection, *The Blues and the Beautiful.* Her work also appears in the literary magazine *Spillwords Press,* on the *Masticadores* platform, as well as in *Tranquility: An Anthology of Haiku* published by Literary Revelations and the 2025 edition of *Sunflower Tanka Anthology - Dreams* compiled by Robbie Cheadle and Colleen M. Chesebro. A nature enthusiast, Nicole also loves exploring the outdoors and capturing images to share on her blogs and on photography sites. Connect with Nicole on her blogs at starrysteps.wordpress.com and doarnicol.wordpress.com (bilingual blog) as well as @nicoles.steps on Instagram.

Phoebe Shade is a 12-year-old artist based in Austin, Texas, who enjoys working in both digital and traditional media. Her first published works—a poem titled *Magic Doors* and an acrylic painting titled *Stargazing Cat on a Beach at Midnight*—appeared in *Poems for Tomorrow,* Issue 3 and in Collaborature Literary Journal. She enjoys creating art that blends imagination with real-life experiences. When she's not creating, she can usually be found listening to records, playing the drums, thrifting, or tracking down the best ramen and sushi spots in town.

Merril D. Smith is a Pushcart-nominated poet who writes from southern New Jersey. Her work has been published widely in journals and anthologies. Her full-length poetry collection, *River Ghosts* (Nightingale & Sparrow Press), was Black Bough Poetry's December 2022 Book of the Month. Her new collection, *Held Inside the Folds of Time* (Jane's Studio Press), was released in autumn 2025. Find her at Bluesky: @merrildsmith.bsky.social; Instagram: @mdsmithnj; Blog: merrildsmith.org.

Edward St. James is a writer and poet living in New York. He can be found on BlueSky.

Joshua Walker is The Last Bard, an independent poet with over 310,000 followers across platforms. His work has appeared in *Potomac Review, South Florida Poetry Journal, Solarpunk Magazine,* and more. Drawing from life with schizoaffective disorder, he writes in a voice both raw and defiant, finding resilience in imperfection. Refusing institutional ties, Walker stands as a fully freelance poet, carrying forward a tradition of truth-telling, survival, and resistance through poetry.

Eileen "ike" West, MA, is an international teacher and writer featured in Susan Smit's *Wise Women* (NL, 2003) and Susan Taylor's *Sexual Radiance* (US, 1998). Across decades, West's essays liberally sprinkle magazines and other publications in the US, UK, and EU. Samples are available at ikewest.com. West's first poetry collection, *Whistler of Petty Crimes* (2023), and her earlier novels, *Away from Hannah's Castle* (US/NL, 2006) and *Another Giant World* (UK, 2018), are available through various and sundry outlets.

Kim Whysall-Hammond is a Londoner who now lives in the English countryside. She worked in climate research and the technical side of telecommunications and is a geek—except she forgets a lot. Her poetry has appeared in *Black Nore Review, Dreich, Littoral,* and *The Martello,* as well as magazines in the US and Canada. She also has poems in anthologies from Arachne Press, Brigids Gate Press, Milk and Cake Press, and Palewell Press. She won third prize in the 2023 Dwarf Star Speculative Poetry Award. Her debut pamphlet, *Messages from the Road,* was published by Palewell Press in autumn 2024.

Meghan Woodward is a poet and app developer who lives in Seattle, Washington. She has not been published in 20 years (since college) and is prolifically sharing her work (though not this piece) on Bluesky.

Acknowledgments & Gratitude

First and foremost, this collection wouldn't exist without the generosity, honesty, and vulnerability of the poets who shared their work. Each of you offered a glimpse into what it means to endure, adapt, and keep showing up. Through humor, grief, reflection, and resilience, your voices create a space where healing and hope coexist. Thank you for trusting us with your words.

Several poems in this collection first appeared elsewhere:

"It's All about Death, Really" by Barbara Harris Leonhard first appeared in *Well Versed 2022: A Collection of Poetry and Prose.*

"Black Moments" by Nicole Sara was previously published in *Chewers by Masticadores* (2025) and in her collection *The Blues and the Beautiful* (2025).

"Paradise is" by Nicole Sara was previously published in *Spillwords Press* (2022) and in her collection *The Blues and the Beautiful* (2025).

"Flood," "I Think We Should Have Some Make-Believe," and "A Protest Piece" by Erica Johnson first appeared on ethicalela.com as part of their ongoing Open Write for Educators series.

The opening epigraph from Jeff Tweedy, drawn from an interview in *MOJO Magazine* (June 21, 2025), appears with gratitude for his reminder to "double-down on beauty" when the world feels unsteady.

The opening epigraph from Leonard Cohen's "Anthem," and the closing epigraph from Wendell Berry's "The Real Work," appear with appreciation and respect for their original authors.

Special thanks to the contributors who shared not only poems, but the stories and emotions behind them—and to everyone who continues to believe that art can be both a coping mechanism and a catalyst for connection.

And to Melissa Lemay for generously offering an additional pass on the manuscript during the final proofreading stage—your kindness and attention to detail are truly appreciated.

Any remaining errors or formatting inconsistencies are ours alone. While many offered invaluable input throughout the process, we handled the final editing and layout—so if anything slipped through, that's on us.

— Nick Allison and Rachel Armes-McLaughlin,

Postscript (January 8, 2026)

As this book was going to press, news broke of fellow poet Renee Nicole Good, who was gunned down by ICE agents in Minneapolis. She was unarmed and not engaged in any act that posed an immediate threat. Video of the incident circulated widely, intensifying concerns about immigration enforcement, the erosion of due process, and the use of lethal force by federal agents.

Our first collection, *Record of Dissent*, gave voice to resistance in an authoritarian age. *What We Hold On To* turns inward, exploring how we cope, connect, and carry on in uncertain times. Our third collection, tentatively planned for late 2026, is expected to return to our roots in protest and dissent poetry. While the work has not yet begun, it will likely engage topics such as immigration raids, civil liberties, and the human cost of enforcement carried out without transparency or accountability. In moments like this, poetry remains one way to bear witness, to record what is happening, and to refuse silence.

Thank you again for reading. Until we meet again, take care of one another, stay vigilant, and keep showing up.

About The Chaos Section Poetry Project

The Chaos Section Poetry Project grew out of *The Chaos Section*, a long-running opinion site founded in Austin, Texas, in 2012. After publishing essays for years, we wanted to open the door to poetry as well—a way to explore the same world from a different angle and to create room for more voices and forms.

Our first collection, *Record of Dissent*, gave voice to resistance in an authoritarian age. *What We Hold On To* turns inward, exploring how we cope, connect, and carry on in uncertain times.

All of our poetry and prose releases are published under **The Chaos Section Press**.

For updates or to submit work for future publications, visit:
thechaossectionpoetryproject.com

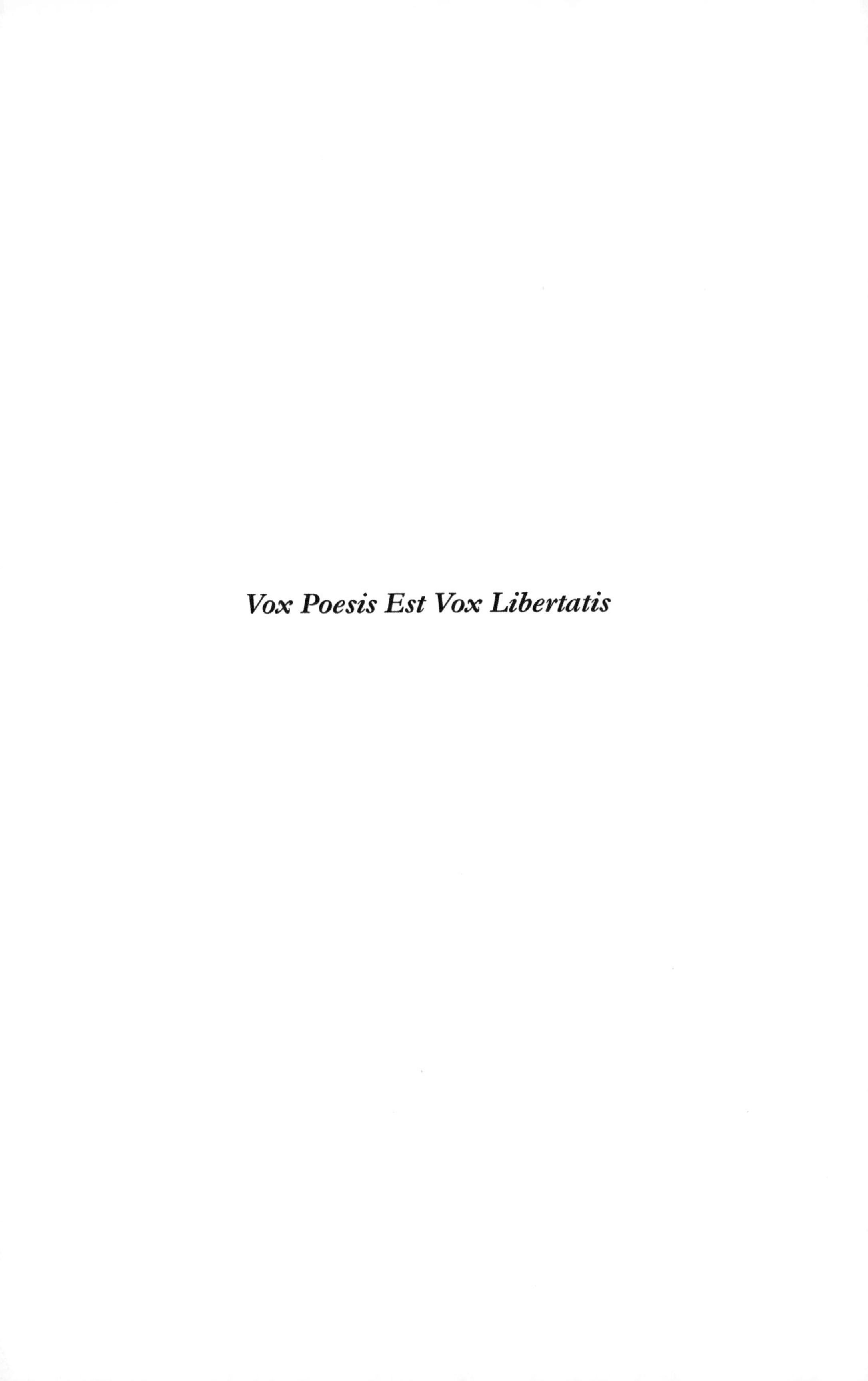

Vox Poesis Est Vox Libertatis

In the DIY, community spirit of *The Chaos Section Poetry Project*, this page is intentionally left blank—for you to write your own poem of coping, connection, or carrying on.

Even if no one ever reads your poem but you, your voice belongs here, too. If you do decide to share, we'd love to see it—post your poem (or a photo of this page) on Bluesky and tag us @chaossectionpoetry.bsky.social.